S is for Smithsonian®

America's Museum Alphabet

Smithsonian Institution

Marie Smith

Written by Marie and Roland Smith

Illustrated by Gijsbert van Frankenhuyzen

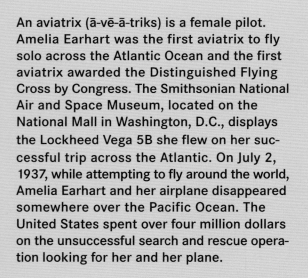

An aviatrix (ā-vē-ā-triks) is a female pilot. Amelia Earhart was the first aviatrix to fly solo across the Atlantic Ocean and the first aviatrix awarded the Distinguished Flying Cross by Congress. The Smithsonian National Air and Space Museum, located on the National Mall in Washington, D.C., displays the Lockheed Vega 5B she flew on her successful trip across the Atlantic. On July 2, 1937, while attempting to fly around the world, Amelia Earhart and her airplane disappeared somewhere over the Pacific Ocean. The United States spent over four million dollars on the unsuccessful search and rescue operation looking for her and her plane.

Another **A**—airplane. The Wright Flyer, the world's first successful airplane, invented and built by Wilbur and Orville Wright has been displayed in the Smithsonian since 1948. It almost didn't make it to the Smithsonian. Orville Wright loaned his flying machine to the Science Museum in London because the Smithsonian refused to acknowledge the Wright brothers as the true inventors of the airplane. The Smithsonian finally gave them credit in 1942. Orville Wright died in 1948 and willed the Wright Flyer to the Smithsonian.

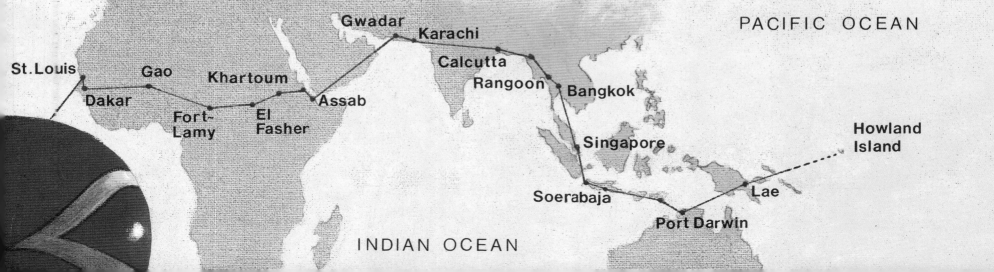

A is for Amelia Earhart,
an aviatrix who pioneered
women's aviation
before she disappeared.

PACIFIC OCEAN

St. Louis

Dakar

Gao

Khartoum

Gwadar

Karachi

Calcutta

Rangoon

Bangkok

Fort-
Lamy

El
Fasher

Assab

Singapore

Howland
Island

Soerabaja

Lae

Port Darwin

INDIAN OCEAN

B is for the Band,
     trombone, trumpet, and tuba.
Instruments making music
          composed by John Philip Sousa.

John Philip Sousa was born in Washington, D.C. His father was a member of the U.S. Marine Band and taught him to play musical instruments. He joined the U.S. Marine Band as an apprentice when he was 13, and promoted to conductor at age 25. He started his own civilian band and became one of the most famous band conductors and composers in the world. He composed the official march of the United States, *The Stars and Stripes Forever!* The silver-tipped baton he used during his concerts is in the National Museum of American History along with some of his musical recordings. The Smithsonian's National Postal Museum has the John Philip Sousa two-cent stamp issued May 3, 1940.

B is for Bracero program. *Bracero* is Spanish for "day laborer." The program was an agreement between the Mexican and the United States governments that brought Mexican men into the United States to work temporarily on food crops and on railroads during World War II. The program had an impact on how agricultural work was done, on migration patterns, and creating Mexican-American communities.

Besides all the exhibits in each of the Smithsonian museums, the Smithsonian has traveling exhibits that are loaned out to cities across the country. "Bittersweet Harvest: The Bracero program 1942-1964" is one of the traveling exhibits with photos of the braceros while on their journey to the United States along with personal interviews.

Bb

C is for Castle,
known for the color red.
Here the Smithsonian started
and continues to spread.

The Smithsonian Information Center, commonly referred to as the "Castle," opened in 1855. No one knew at that time the Smithsonian would grow and expand to include 19 museums, 156 affiliate museums, 9 research centers, 136 million objects, artworks, specimens, libraries, traveling exhibits, and a Web site used all over the world. Designed by James Renwick Jr., the building with its nine towers is made of red sandstone.

A group of people appointed by Congress, called a board of regents, govern the Smithsonian. It includes: the vice president of the United States, chief justice of the Supreme Court, three members of the Senate, three members of Congress, and nine private citizens. The chief executive officer of the Smithsonian is called the secretary. Part of the second floor of the Castle was home to the first secretary, Joseph Henry, and his family. Ten years after it was built fire destroyed sections of the Castle and many valuable items were damaged or destroyed. It took two years to repair. Today the Castle is used for administration and a place for tourists to gather information and highlights about the Smithsonian museums.

D is for the Doll Family.
They have their own house.
Mom and Dad with ten children;
let's look for a mouse!

Faith Bradford was raised in the Washington, D.C. area. She started playing with dollhouses when she was seven years old and continued for over fifty years. She created a dollhouse representing life in the early 1900s for the Doll family. Mr. and Mrs. Doll had ten children—including twins Timmy and Jimmy. Visiting grandparents, servants, and pets helped fill up the 23 rooms of this five-story house. Most of the pieces were collected in Washington, D.C. or handmade by Faith Bradford and her friends. In 1951 Faith gave the Doll family and the dollhouse to the Smithsonian. It is displayed in the Smithsonian's National Museum of American History.

The National Museum of American History was the sixth Smithsonian building to open on the National Mall. Only about 5 to 8 percent of the three million objects in the museum's collection are displayed at a time.

D is also for design. The Cooper-Hewitt National Design Museum is located in the historic Andrew Carnegie Mansion in New York City. The museum focuses on historical and contemporary design.

E e

Big is the word that comes to mind when you enter the National Museum of Natural History. The four-story-high rotunda is home to the world's largest mounted African elephant. It stands over 13 feet tall surrounded by the grasses and plants common to Angola, a country in southern Africa where it once roamed. Across the rotunda is Sant Ocean Hall, the largest exhibit area of the museum. A replica of a 45-foot long right whale, one of the rarest of all marine life animals, hangs from the ceiling. It is modeled after a living whale called Phoenix found in the North Atlantic. A 24-foot high giant squid appears lifelike suspended in a 1,800-gallon tank of nontoxic clear fluid called Novec. Located in dinosaur hall is a 87-foot *diplodocus longus* displayed with a *triceratops* and other dinosaur skeletons.

The National Museum of Natural History, established in 1910, is the largest Smithsonian museum and research unit. Over six million people visit each year, making it the most visited natural history museum in the world.

Elephant from Africa
starts with the letter **E**.
In the Museum of Natural History
it's the first thing to see.

Ff

F is for First Ladies
wearing a special dress,
celebrating at a ball
their husbands' success.

In 1809 Dolley Madison threw a party to honor her husband, James Madison, for his election as the fourth president of the United States. Since then, formal parties called a Presidential Inaugural Ball or Reception have been held to celebrate a president's term of office. The First Ladies' exhibit in the National Museum of American History has many of the dresses worn by presidents' wives for these special occasions. It is one of the most popular exhibits in the museum. George Washington, our first president, did not have an inaugural ball, but one of the gowns his wife Martha wore for other events is part of the collection.

F is also for flag. The most cherished item displayed in the National Museum of American History is the Star-Spangled Banner. It is the flag that flew over Fort McHenry in Baltimore, Maryland, during the War of 1812 with Great Britain. It inspired Francis Scott Key to write a poem that, after being added to music, became our national anthem.

Artist George Catlin traveled thousands of miles from 1830 to 1836 studying Indian tribes living west of the Mississippi River. Hundreds of his paintings depicting the Native American culture and traditions researched during his travels are part of the Smithsonian American Art Museum collection. Some can be found in the Luce Foundation Center on the third floor of the museum. The Luce Center holds over 3,300 pieces of artwork.

G is for the Grand Salon, a spacious space used for a changing display of American artists' work. George Catlin has been one of those artists. It is on the second floor of the Renwick Gallery, which is a branch of the Smithsonian American Art Museum. The Renwick Gallery is across the street from the White House and named after James Renwick Jr., the architect who designed the building. It is home to America's craft and decorative arts from the nineteenth to the twenty-first century.

G is for George Catlin.
His paintings remain
an illustrated record of
Indians from the Plains.

Gg

H is for the Hope Diamond,
surrounded in mystery.
No one knows for sure
this blue jewel's history.

On display at the National Museum of Natural History in the Janet Annenberg Hooker Hall of Geology, Gems, and Minerals is a 45.52 carat, blue diamond called the Hope Diamond. The diamond was discovered in India and sold to the King of France in 1668. It was stolen from the French Crown Jewels during the French Revolution. The diamond is named after Henry Philip Hope, who obtained the diamond sometime before 1839, but exactly when, where or how remains a mystery. Evalyn Walsh McLean from Virginia became owner of the blue diamond for over 35 years.

The jewelry firm of Harry Winston bought it from the McLean estate and in 1958 donated it to the Smithsonian. Harry Winston sent the Hope Diamond to the Smithsonian through the United States mail! It arrived in a box wrapped in plain brown paper—insured for a million dollars. It is one of the most visited items in any museum in the world.

h

H

I is for Insect zoo.
    Take time to explore.
  It has a beehive
      with its own back door.

The second floor of the National Museum of Natural History is home to the O. Orkin Insect Zoo. This special zoo has a live beehive with its own exit to the outside. Worker bees fly back and forth, providing nectar and pollen for the queen and hive. Bees, like all insects, are invertebrates with six legs and segmented bodies—the head, thorax, and abdomen.

Insects are the largest and most diverse group of the animal kingdom. The National Museum of Natural History has over 35 million insect specimens in its collection. Only a small percentage are on display; most are kept in special preservation drawers.

If you want to work at the insect zoo you should study to be an entomologist. They are scientists who collect insects, identify new species, and study their relationships with the rest of the natural world. The entomology staff at the National Museum of Natural History has about 50 full-time employees, 30 resident research associates, students, and volunteers. Many different kinds of scientists work at the Smithsonian.

J j

J is for Justice Thurgood Marshall,
who fought for school desegregation;
became the first African-American
on the highest court of our nation.

In front of the Smithsonian Anacostia Community Museum stands a sculpture symbolizing the life and work of Thurgood Marshall titled *Real Justice: the Spirit of Thurgood Marshall*, by Allen Uzikee Nelson. Thurgood Marshall was born on July 2, 1908, and raised in Baltimore, Maryland. His great-grandfather was a slave; his father worked at an all-white country club and his mother was a teacher. When he applied to the law school at the University of Maryland he was refused entry because he was African-American. Instead he went to Howard University graduating with honors. He led the legal team for the Brown v. Board of Education case brought before the U.S. Supreme Court that resulted in a landmark ruling ending segregated schooling in 1954. Marshall became the first African-American Justice of the Supreme Court in 1967. After his death on January 24, 1993, he was awarded our country's highest civilian honor, the Presidential Medal of Freedom.

Anacostia Community Museum, started in 1967, is not on the National Mall. It is a Smithsonian museum located in the southeast area of the District of Columbia and named after the historic Anacostia neighborhood.

Every year the Smithsonian has a kite festival on the National Mall. Paul E. Garber, founder of the Smithsonian National Air and Space Museum started the festival in 1967. Paul Garber grew up loving kites and anything to do with aviation. He was lucky to receive kite-handling tips from inventor Alexander Graham Bell and to have seen Orville Wright fly the world's first military airplane at Fort Myer, Virginia. His childhood hobby became important during World War II when he successfully helped train gunners for battle using his invention of a diamond-shaped kite with pictures of enemy aircraft for target practice. Over 350,000 of the diamond-shaped target kites were made.

Paul Garber started working for the Smithsonian in 1920 and continued working in different positions for 72 years. He traveled the world searching for aviation treasures for the museum. One of his most important additions to the museum was the Wright brother's flyer in 1948.

K
k

The annual kite festival—
a colorful display
flying above the National Mall.
Kites start with the letter K.

WHITES ONLY

WE SERVE WHITES only

COLORED WAITING ROOM

L is for Lunch counter.
Four students were silent
in a protest they chose
to be nonviolent.

The historic Woolworth lunch counter from Greensboro, North Carolina, is in the National Museum of American History. Racial segregation ended in United States schools in 1954 but racial segregation was still legal in public areas such as motels, restaurants, movie theaters, swimming pools, and even at drinking fountains.

On February 1, 1960, four African-American college students sat down at a whites-only lunch counter at the Woolworth store in Greensboro and were refused service. When asked to leave, they quietly remained in their seats waiting to be served. Their nonviolent sit-in drew national attention. Soon sit-ins were staged at other lunch counters and other public areas that would not serve African-Americans. These nonviolent protests helped to pass the Civil Rights Act of 1964, outlawing racial segregation in public areas. A section of the lunch counter from Greensboro was donated to the Smithsonian when the Woolworth store closed in 1993.

L is also for libraries. The Smithsonian Institution Libraries have 20 branch libraries located in Smithsonian museums, research centers, and offices in Washington, D.C., New York City, Maryland, and the Republic of Panama.

Ll

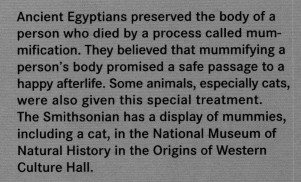

Mm

Ancient Egyptians preserved the body of a person who died by a process called mummification. They believed that mummifying a person's body promised a safe passage to a happy afterlife. Some animals, especially cats, were also given this special treatment. The Smithsonian has a display of mummies, including a cat, in the National Museum of Natural History in the Origins of Western Culture Hall.

M is also for modern art. The Hirshhorn Museum and Sculpture Garden has over 12,000 pieces of modern and contemporary art in its collection. The round donut-like structure sets it apart from the more traditional buildings on the mall.

Another **M** is for music. The National Museum of American History has a collection of music covering all the diverse groups that have made the United States their home. Smithsonian Folkway Recordings is a nonprofit record label of the institution. Songs can be listened to from the Smithsonian Web page.

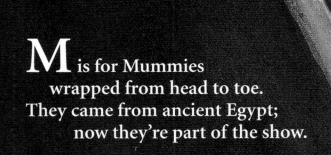

M is for Mummies
wrapped from head to toe.
They came from ancient Egypt;
now they're part of the show.

N n

N is for Nestwatch.
Do you know the reason
some birds stay all year round;
some just stay a season?

Birds migrate in the spring and the fall flying long distances in search of food, water, and shelter. But not all birds migrate. Some birds find enough food to stay in one area over the winter. The Smithsonian's Neighborhood Nestwatch program invites people to be backyard biologists. Scientists want to know if these backyard birds are successful in reproducing, if the birds come back to their nests, and how long these birds live. Neighborhood Nestwatch volunteers are asked to observe bird activity to help find answers to these questions. They report their observations back to the Neighborhood Nestwatch at the Migratory Bird Center.

Dr. Peter P. Marra of the Smithsonian Migratory Bird Center started Neighborhood Nestwatch, which is based at the Smithsonian's National Zoological Park. Dr. Marra is an ornithologist and ecologist. An ornithologist is a scientist that studies birds. An ecologist is someone that studies the lives of animals, in this case birds, in their natural environment.

Owney was a stray dog that made himself at home in a post office in Albany, New York. He began following mailbags wherever they went—on wagons, trains, even ships, always returning to the Albany Post Office. Mail clerks at the post offices he visited began placing tags on his collar showing where he had been. The clerks in Albany collected over 200 tags from across the United States. Owney became the unofficial good luck mascot of the Railway Mail Service. He was so loved that when he died he was preserved by a taxidermist and is on display at the Smithsonian's National Postal Museum. The museum is located in the historic Washington, D.C. Post Office Building, less than a mile away from the National Mall.

Protecting the mail is the job of postal inspectors with the United States Postal Inspection Service. Postmaster General Benjamin Franklin started the service in 1776. They are sometimes referred to as the Silent Service because they turn away from public recognition. Find out more about their important service to our country at the Smithsonian's National Postal Museum Web site.

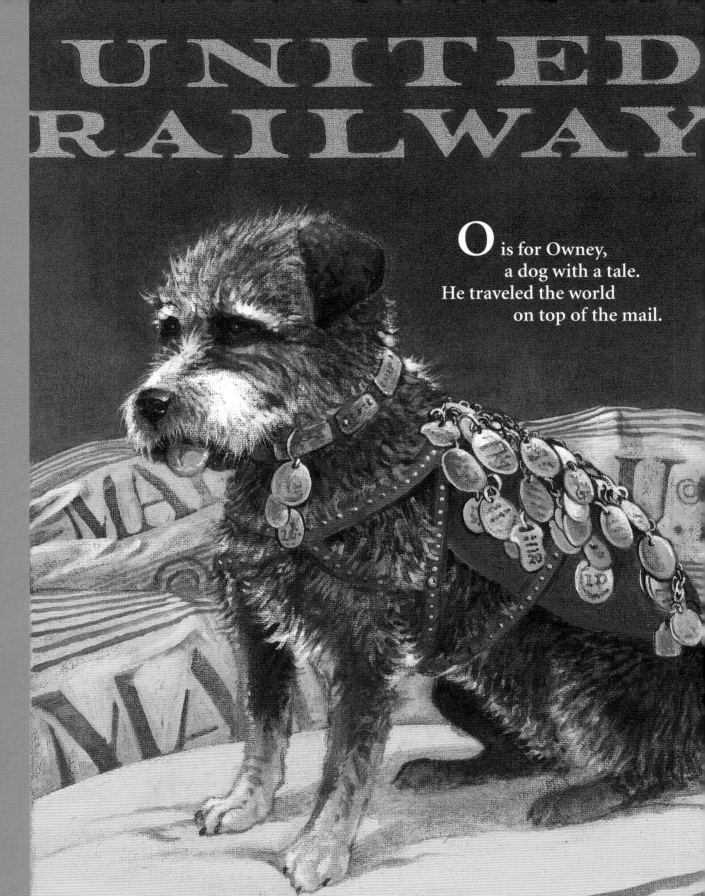

O is for Owney,
a dog with a tale.
He traveled the world
on top of the mail.

UNITED RAILWAY

P is for Peacocks
painted on a wall.
Harmony in Blue and Gold,
a Princess standing tall.

P p

The Freer Gallery of Art opened in 1923 and was the first Smithsonian museum for fine arts. A popular room of the gallery is Harmony in Blue and Gold: The Peacock Room. Originally it was a dining room in a London home designed and painted by James Whistler for wealthy shipbuilder Frederick Leyland. Over the fireplace was a painting called *La Princesse du pays de la porcelaine* of Whistler's (The Princess from the land of porcelain). After Leyland died, the room was sold to Charles Freer, taken apart, and shipped to his home in Detroit, Michigan. Freer collected Asian art and eventually gave his entire collection, including the Peacock Room, to the Smithsonian.

P is also for the Patent Office Building located a short distance from the National Mall. During the Civil War it was a temporary barracks, hospital, and morgue. In 1877 a fire destroyed parts of the upper floors along with 87,000 patent models. In 1968 the Historic Landmark Building became the Donald W. Reynolds Center for American Art and Portraiture, home for the Smithsonian American Art Museum, the National Portrait Gallery, the Lunder Conservation Center, and the Luce Foundation.

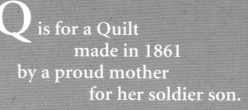

Q is for a Quilt
　　　made in 1861
by a proud mother
　　　for her soldier son.

Quilts have been made in many parts of the world using needlework techniques that have been practiced for centuries. In the United States, it has become a popular form of American Folk Art. Americans have produced beautiful, interesting, and historically significant quilts influencing quiltmaking throughout the world.

During the Civil War women pieced together quilts to help raise money for the war effort and keep loved ones warm. Specifically made to be long and narrow fitting a soldier's cot, they could easily be folded, rolled up, and carried like a sling.

Mary Rockhold Teter of Noblesville, Indiana made a patriotic quilt with a stars-and-stripes pattern for her son George. Names of the Union generals he served were stitched into the stars. The Smithsonian received the quilt from Mary's great-grandson, Eugene Teter, in 1940.

The Smithsonian National Quilt Collection has over 400 quilts from the eighteenth through the twentieth century, most of them made in the United States. Kept in a temperature and humidity controlled room, each quilt is in a separate drawer in a dust-resistant cabinet.

When someone hears the words Dorothy, a scarecrow, a tin man, or cowardly lion, most people think of the 1939 film *The Wizard of Oz*. Dorothy, lost in the magical Land of Oz, finally discovers the key to returning to Kansas is clicking her ruby slippers together and saying "there's no place like home." The famous slippers are on display at the National Museum of American History. At least four pair of the size 5 ruby slippers were made for actress Judy Garland who played in the movie. The pair on display was sent to the Smithsonian as an anonymous gift.

R is also for red—the red sweater worn by Fred Rogers, creator, producer, and host of "Mr. Rogers' Neighborhood." It was knitted by his mother and given to the museum on November 20, 1984. It is in the Smithsonian archives. With limited space and a need to conserve objects, curators and museum executives often make decisions to rotate or remove objects on exhibit. This helps the historic objects to last for future generations.

R **r**

R is for the Road
Dorothy traveled with friends.
Follow the yellow bricks—
Land of Oz is where it ends.

S s

James Smithson, an English scientist, willed his fortune to his nephew with an unusual condition. If his nephew should die without heirs, then his fortune should go "to the United States of America, to found at Washington, under the name of the Smithsonian Institution, an establishment for the increase and diffusion of knowledge among men." His nephew died without family so Smithson's fortune, changed into 105 bags of gold, was shipped to the United States.

Senator John Calhoun of South Carolina wanted to give the treasure back, saying it was beneath the dignity of the United States to accept money from an unknown Englishman. John Quincy Adams, former president then senator, argued to keep it. After years of debate with a vote of 26 to 13 the Senate passed an act organizing the Smithsonian Institution. President James Polk signed it into law.

Smithson died on June 27, 1829, and 75 years after his death his body was brought to the United States and placed in a special crypt in the Smithsonian Castle. No one knows why he gave his fortune to the United States.

S is for Smithson.
Congress was shocked when told
his gift to the United States:
one hundred and five bags of gold!

T is for Tin Lizzie,
built by Henry Ford.
His dream was to make a car
Americans could afford.

The Smithsonian National Museum of American History has 73 cars on display, on loan, or in storage. One of the cars is the Model T known as the Tin Lizzie. It was built by Henry Ford, an inventor and entrepreneur, who started moving assembly lines and the mass production of cars in the United States. More than 15 million Model T's were sold from 1908 to 1927. During World War II Henry Ford used his factories for the war effort and produced bombers, Jeeps, and tanks.

The museum also has Richard Petty's stock car that he drove on his 200th NASCAR™ victory at the Talladega Speedway in Alabama on July 4, 1984. It was the first NASCAR™ stock car added to the museum's collection.

Not a car but something with wheels is Ed Roberts' motorized wheelchair. The wheelchair has a headlight for nighttime travel and a special seat for comfort. Roberts, who was paralyzed by polio, started the first independent-living centers for disabled people in the United States and traveled the world campaigning for disability rights. Friends who wanted to honor his life donated his chair to the Smithsonian after his death in 1995.

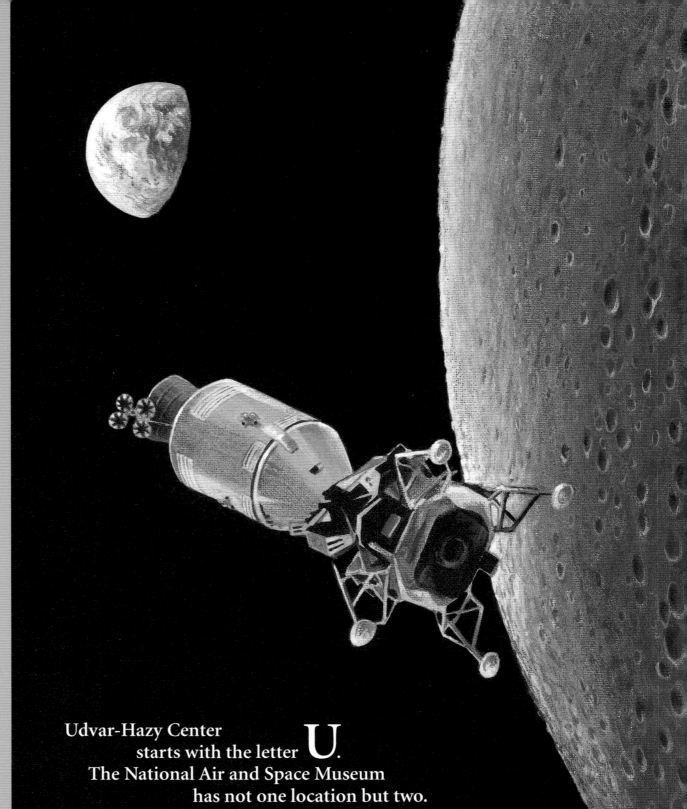

On July 16, 1969, Michael Collins, Neil Armstrong, and Edwin "Buzz" Aldrin took a trip to the Moon in the Apollo 11 Command Module *Columbia*. Neil Armstrong and Edwin Aldrin became the first men to walk on the Moon. They spent over two hours on the Moon's surface gathering data and samples before climbing back into the *Columbia* for the trip to Earth. After they landed safely in the Pacific Ocean, they spent time in a mobile quarantine facility on board the USS *Hornet* making sure they had not brought back any Moon germs. The Smithsonian's National Air and Space Museum has two locations; one on the National Mall, and another, the Steven F. Udvar-Hazy Center, in Chantilly, Virginia. The Udvar-Hazy Center has many artifacts from the historic journey to the Moon, including the Mobile Quarantine Facility.

U is also for underground. The Sackler Gallery, Freer Gallery, and the National Museum of African Art are underground and connected by a tunnel. The National Museum of African Art opened in 1987. Some of the African art collection on display was from the Walt Disney Company, originally planned as a display at the Epcot Center.

Udvar-Hazy Center
starts with the letter U.
The National Air and Space Museum
has not one location but two.

V is for Volunteers.
        There is plenty of opportunity
if you want to help and become part of
        the Smithsonian community.

A volunteer might welcome you as you enter a Smithsonian museum or answer the phone when you call with a question. A volunteer might be the one who leads a tour or gives a demonstration. They may work in the many gardens of the Smithsonian. They also may work behind the scenes with the Smithsonian staff. There are about 6,500 volunteers working at the Smithsonian.

The first secretary, Joseph Henry, recruited the first volunteers at the Smithsonian in the late 1840s. Some of these early volunteers worked across the nation collecting weather reports and sending the information to the Smithsonian. This important volunteer work led to the beginning of the first National Weather Service.

Volunteers since then continue to be an important part of the workforce of the Smithsonian. Some are also called docents, who receive special training and make a time commitment to be part of the Smithsonian.

V
V

The Wizard of Menlo Park—
A man whose invention
is the reason under **W**
we give him special mention.

W
W
W

Thomas Edison was named the Wizard of Menlo Park after he invented the phonograph. The first song he recorded was "Mary Had a Little Lamb." You may also know him for his invention of the lightbulb or his work with electricity. He had over 1,093 patents—more than anyone else in the world. Menlo Park, New Jersey was home for his "Invention Factory." Thomas Edison and other inventors' stories can be found in the Lemelson Center located in the National Museum of American History.

W is also for Web site. If you do not have a chance to visit the Lemelson Center in the National Museum of American History, the National Museum of Natural History, the National Air and Space Museum, or any of the Smithsonian museums in person, go to the Smithsonian Web site for a virtual tour or blog discussion, check out YouTube, Flicker, Facebook, Twitter, or watch the Smithsonian Channel on television. You can explore all the programs the Smithsonian offers and have fun looking at the diverse and unique items collected since it opened.

Xu Bing is an artist who grew up in China during the Cultural Revolution. He studied calligraphy, the art of producing decorative handwriting or lettering with a brush or pen. He received a master's degree from the Central Academy of Fine Art in Beijing. His sculpture *Monkeys grasping for the moon* at the Arthur M. Sackler Gallery is a version of a Buddhist folktale. A monkey looking down a well sees the moon in the water below. He cries for help to get the moon out. His friends link arms and tails together to form a chain, finding at the bottom of the well only the moon's reflection. They realize that the things we work hardest to achieve may prove to be only an illusion. The sculpture creates the word for monkey in over a dozen languages.

Xu Bing's sculpture hangs in the glass-covered atrium, cascading down the stairwell to the third-level reflecting pool of the Arthur M. Sackler Gallery, which is part of the National Museum of Asian Art.

X
x

X is for Xu Bing, a sculptor who made the display *Monkeys grasping for the moon* in the Sackler Gallery stairway.

Yy

People called Yupik starts with the letter Y.
They live underneath the aurora borealis
that lights up the northern sky.

The aurora borealis is the colorful light show that flashes across the northern sky. Alaska Native people live in the arctic region area where the northern lights are easily seen. The Alaska Natives have 11 distinct cultures and speak different languages and dialects. Some are called Yupik and Iñupiaq. They have lived in the north coast and Seward Peninsula, St. Lawrence Island and coastal Chukotka areas of Alaska for over 10,000 years. Their ancestors developed skills in weaving, sewing, hunting, and carving that helped them survive the snow and ice surrounding them most of the year. Today many carry on their native traditions.

Other native groups are Yup'ik and Cup'ik who live in the southwest mainland area of Alaska. They are skilled in hunting and fishing. Their ancestors moved with the seasons for hunting, fishing, and gathering of plants.

The National Museum of the American Indian was the 16th to be added to the Smithsonian and is located on the National Mall. Native architects and consultants worked on the design and layout. The museum has over 800,000 items highlighting 12,000 years of native history from the Western Hemisphere and Hawaii. The George Gustav Heye Center located in New York City is also part of the National Museum of the American Indian.

Z is for Zoo.
Pandas eating bamboo,
a gift from China
back in 1972.

Zz

The Smithsonian's National Zoological Park is located inside Rock Creek Park in Washington, D.C. More than 2,000 animals live at the National Zoo. The National Zoo has scientists in field stations located around the world and a research and conservation center in Front Royal, Virginia.

Ling Ling and Hsing Hsing were a gift to the United States from the People's Republic of China in 1972 and lived at the National Zoo until thier deaths. Giant Pandas Tian Tian and Mei Xiang were sent from China on a loan program and on July 9, 2005, became parents of panda cub Tai Shan. His name means "peaceful mountain."

Giant Pandas are found in the cool bamboo forests in the mountains of China. Cubs weigh four to six ounces at birth and can grow up to 250 pounds eating mostly bamboo. Because so few of these gentle-looking creatures are found in the wild they are listed as endangered.

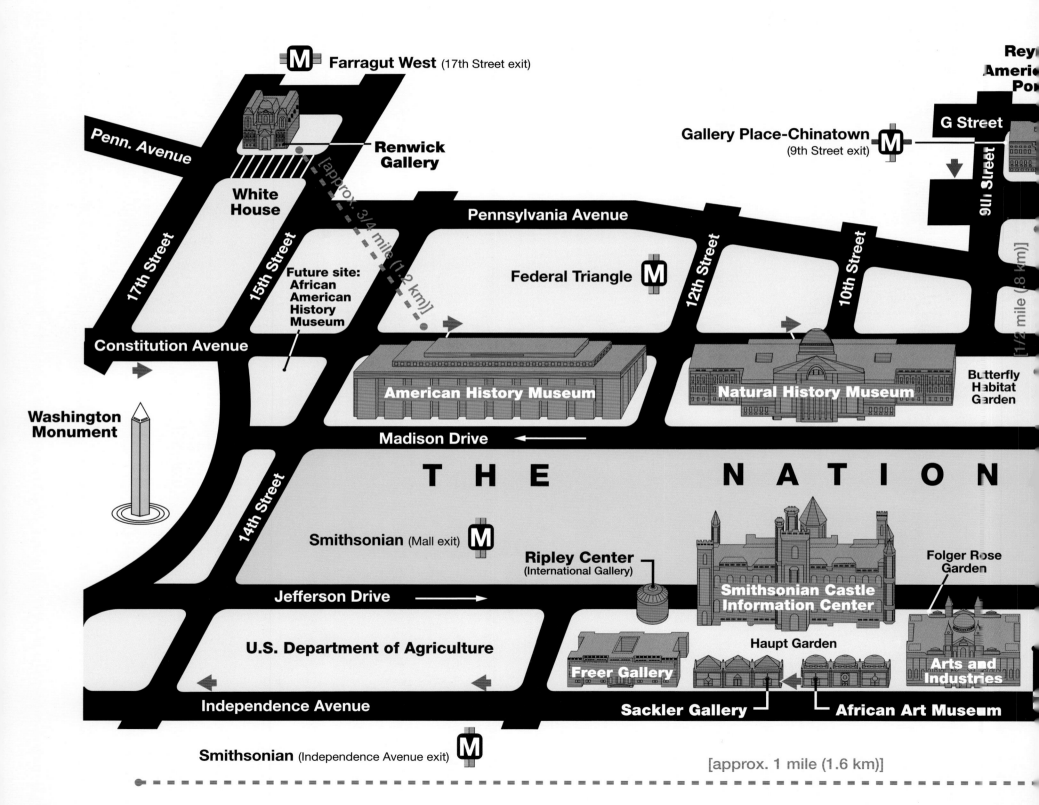

M Farragut West (17th Street exit)

Gallery Place-Chinatown M
(9th Street exit)

G Street

Penn. Avenue

Renwick
Gallery

9th Street

White
House

Pennsylvania Avenue

17th Street

15th Street

Future site:
African
American
History
Museum

Federal Triangle M

12th Street

10th Street

Constitution Avenue

Butterfly
Habitat
Garden

American History Museum

Natural History Museum

Washington
Monument

Madison Drive ←

THE   NATION

14th Street

Smithsonian (Mall exit) M

Ripley Center
(International Gallery)

Folger Rose
Garden

Smithsonian Castle
Information Center

Jefferson Drive →

U.S. Department of Agriculture

Haupt Garden

Arts and
Industries

Freer Gallery

Independence Avenue

Sackler Gallery

African Art Museum

Smithsonian (Independence Avenue exit) M

[approx. 1 mile (1.6 km)]

[approx. 3/4 mile (1.2 km)]

[1/2 mile (.8 km)]

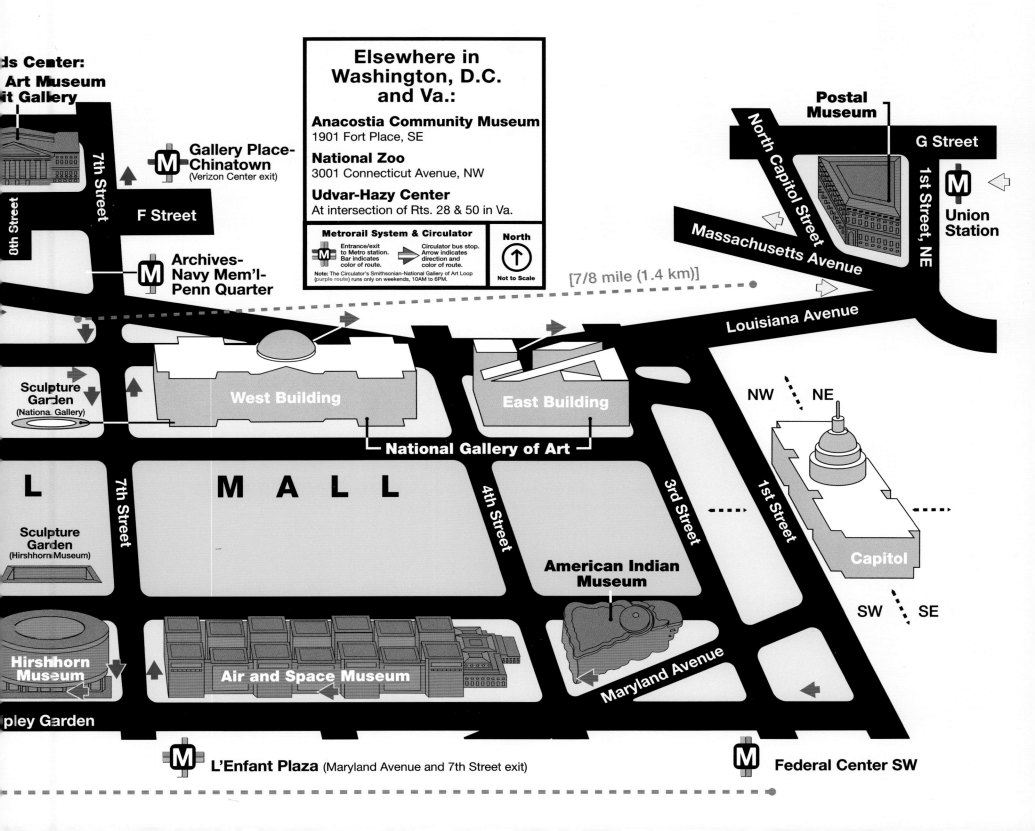

near the National Mall in Washington, D.C.

Elsewhere in Washington, D.C. and Va.:

Anacostia Community Museum
1901 Fort Place, SE

National Zoo
3001 Connecticut Avenue, NW

Udvar-Hazy Center
At intersection of Rts. 28 & 50 in Va.

Metrorail System & Circulator

Ⓜ Entrance/exit to Metro station. Bar indicates color of route.

➡ Circulator bus stop. Arrow indicates direction and color of route.

Note: The Circulator's Smithsonian-National Gallery of Art Loop (purple route) runs only on weekends, 10AM to 6PM.

North
↑
Not to Scale

ds Center:
Art Museum
it Gallery

0th Street

7th Street

Ⓜ **Gallery Place-Chinatown**
(Verizon Center exit)

F Street

Ⓜ **Archives-Navy Mem'l-Penn Quarter**

Postal Museum

North Capitol Street

Massachusetts Avenue

G Street

1st Street, NE

Ⓜ **Union Station**

[7/8 mile (1.4 km)]

Louisiana Avenue

Sculpture Garden
(National Gallery)

West Building

East Building

National Gallery of Art

NW NE

L

7th Street

MALL

4th Street

3rd Street

1st Street

Capitol

Sculpture Garden
(Hirshhorn Museum)

American Indian Museum

SW SE

Hirshhorn Museum

Air and Space Museum

Maryland Avenue

pley Garden

Ⓜ **L'Enfant Plaza** (Maryland Avenue and 7th Street exit)

Ⓜ **Federal Center SW**

For Bethany and Lee who gave us John and Will, two wonderful reasons to visit the Smithsonian.

Love,
AHNA AND GRAMPS

❧

To all docents and volunteers.

GIJSBERT

ILLUSTRATOR'S ACKNOWLEDGMENTS

To Xu Bing, Casey Tang, and Jesse Coffino-Greenberg. Thanks for the working photos. To Nancy Springer, docent at the insect zoo, Holly Frakes from Schuler Books and Music, Lansing Civic Players for costume rental, the Henry Ford, Benson Ford Research Center, Greenfield Village, Daishya Stanley, Matthew Spear, and principal Kimberly Johnson Ray of Reo Elementary of Lansing, Michigan, and finally David Geister. Thanks to you all for your invaluable help.

Smithsonian Institution

This trademark is owned by the Smithsonian Institution and is registered in the U.S. Patent and Trademark Office.

Text Copyright © 2010 Marie and Roland Smith
Illustration Copyright © 2010 Gijsbert van Frankenhuyzen

Sleeping Bear Press®
315 E. Eisenhower Parkway, Suite 200
Ann Arbor MI 48108
www.sleepingbearpress.com

© 2010 Sleeping Bear Press is an imprint of Gale, a part of Cengage Learning.

Printed and bound in the United States.

Library of Congress Cataloging-in-Publication Data

Smith, Marie, 1951-
S is for Smithsonian : America's museum alphabet / written by Marie and Roland Smith ; illustrated by Gijsbert van Frankenhuyzen. —1st ed.
p. cm.
ISBN 978-1-58536-314-8
1. Smithsonian Institution—Juvenile literature. 2. Alphabet books—Juvenile literature. I. Smith, Roland, 1951- II. Frankenhuyzen, Gijsbert van, ill. III. Title.
Q11.S8S39 2010
069.09753—dc22   2009043428